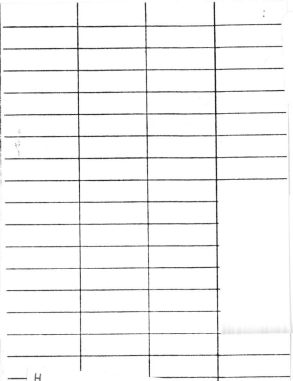

Siskiyou County Schools Library
Yreka, California

MY FIRST
FOURTH OF JULY
BOOK

by Harriet W. Hodgson
illustrated by Linda Hohag

created by The Child's World

CHILDRENS PRESS ®
CHICAGO

Library of Congress Cataloging in Publication Data

Hodgson, Harriet W.
  My first Fourth of July book.

  Summary: A collection of poems about traditional
celebrations of America's independence, describing
picnics, fireworks, and bicycle parades.
  1. Fourth of July—Juvenile poetry. 2. Children's
poetry, American. [1. Fourth of July—Poetry.
2. American poetry] I. Hohag, Linda, ill. II. Title.
PS3558.034346M9 1987   811'.54   86-30987
ISBN 0-516-02907-X

MY FIRST
Fourth of July
BOOK

Happy Birthday, America

Happy birthday, America.
Happy birthday to you.
Fifty states under a flag
Of red, white and blue.

Happy birthday, America.
Happy birthday to you.
I wish the Fourth of July
Were my birthday, too.

Lady of Liberty

Lady of Liberty,
     Lady of Light. . .
Someone is thinking of
     You tonight.

Standing so quiet,
     Standing so tall. . .
A birthday present
     For one and all.

Lady of Liberty,
     Lady of Light. . .
I am thinking of
     You tonight.

The Marching Band

Tap your feet, and clap your hands.
Here it comes. . .the marching band.

First are the drums. Rat-a-tat-tat.
Each tall drummer wears a red hat.

Here are the horns, looking brassy. . .
Wah-oh-wah-wah, sounding sassy.

Tubby tubas with holes on top—
Oom-pa, oom-pa, ooom-pa, pa-pop.

Tap your feet, and clap your hands.
There is goes. . .the marching band.

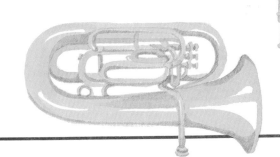

9

Bicycle Parade

Here we go 'round the block again,
  Block again, block again;
Here we go 'round the block again,
  Bicycle parade!
Some have streamers in the spokes,
  In the spokes, in the spokes;
Some have streamers in the spokes,
  Bicycle parade!
Some are tied with big balloons,
  Big balloons, big balloons;
Some are tied with big balloons,
  Bicycle parade!

(Repeat first stanza.)

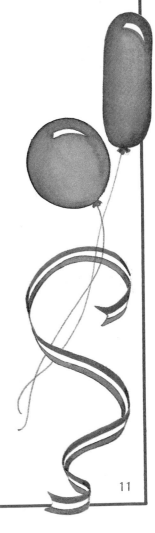

This poem may be sung to the tune of
"Here We Go Round the Mulberry Bush."

Wiggle Worm

Wiggle worm,
Giggle worm
Squiggles JULY.

Then wiggles
A fat 4,
Squiggling by.

Wiggle worm,
Giggle worm
On holiday.

Wiggle worm,
Giggle worm
Squiggles away.

Lemonade Stand

Lemonade for sale. . .by the glass or pail.
Who will buy my lemonade for sale?

This Fourth holiday, my friends are away.
Who will buy my lemonade for sale?

Guess I'll try a sip. (Just a little dip.)
Who will buy my lemonade for sale?

Oh my golly-gosh. Hear my stomach slosh.
Who will buy my lemonade for sale?

Seems I drank it all. So I need not call,
"Who will buy my lemonade for sale?"

Picnics

Ants. Bees. Flies. Fleas. . .
Like to picnic with me.

Ants. Bees. Flies. Fleas. . .
Eat all they can see.

Meat. Chips. Grapes. Dips. . .
All are nibbled fast.

With ants, bees, flies, fleas. . .
Food doesn't last!

Skinny Sparkler

I
hold a
skinny
skinny
skinny
sparkler
which
flares
flares
flares
flashes
flashes
flashes
fizzles
fizzles
fizzles
until it's out out out.

Counting Fireflies

One firefly. Two fireflies.
Three fireflies. Four.
Five fireflies. Six fireflies.
Seven fireflies. More.
Eight fireflies. Nine fireflies.
Ten fireflies. Then. . .
See fireflies. New fireflies.
And start counting again!

(*Read poem again.*)

Hot Dog on a Stick

When is a hot dog,
    Burny spot dog,
When is a hot dog done?

Done when it spurts,
    And when it squirts?
Then is a hot dog done?

Done when it drips,
    And when it slips?
Then is a hot dog done?

When is a hot dog,
    Big black spot dog,
When is a hot dog done?

24

Homemade Ice Cream

Clunk, clunk,
    Goes the ice.
Clunk, clunk.

Squeak, squeak,
    Goes the crank.
Squeak, squeak.

Woosh, woosh,
    Goes the paddle.
Woosh, woosh.

Slurp, slurp,
    Goes my tongue.
Slurp, slurp.

Uncle Sam

Once Uncle Sam was real—
A boy who grew into a man
Named Sam Wilson.
He married, had children,
Owned a business.

Now Uncle Sam is pretend.
Just a picture dressed in flag colors.
A white-haired grandpa with a white beard
Who makes us think of America—
Its land, its towns, its people.

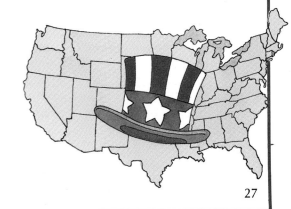

Fireworks

A rocket shoots upwards,
Red sparks trailing
Across an inky sky.
Roman candles flare
Like puff balls,
Booming so hard
My chest wiggles.
More fireworks explode:
Two Stage Jets,
Screaming Meemies,
Whistling Jupiters.
Scary but beautiful
Until the last ones
Crayon the sky with colors
Which turn to night.

(This poem refers to fireworks by their actual names.)

Cheer for America

Read what you want to read;
    See what you want to see.
Cheer for America;
    America is free.

Go where you want to go;
    Own your own property.
Cheer for America;
    America is free.

Say what you want to say;
    Be what you want to be.
Cheer for America;
    America is free!